THE CULTURE KEEPER

The annual Kresge Eminent Artist Award salutes an exceptional artist in the visual, performing or literary arts for lifelong professional achievements and contributions to metropolitan Detroit's cultural community.

Olayami Dabls is the 2022 Kresge Eminent Artist. This monograph honors his life and work.

THE CULTURE KEEPER

OLAYAMI DABLS' GRAND VISION

Nichole M. Christian, creative director and editor
Patrick Barber, art director
with contributions from Aneb Kgositsile,
Marion "Mame" Jackson, Lauren Hood,
Charlene Uresy and Lorcan O'Herlihy

TABLE OF

CONTENTS

FOREWORD

I n January 2022, for the 14th time, a Kresge Eminent Artist was recognized for a lifetime of achievements in metropolitan Detroit.

We recognize excellence . . . contributions to their art forms . . . and, most importantly, contributions to our cultural community.

Collectively, the artists of past years have given us murals, as much as 11 stories high, and worked the alchemy of earth and fire to create stunning ceramics that you can hold in your hands. They've frozen our times for posterity through photographs and have made the air around us pulsate with music. They've made words dance on the page and images dance on canvas.

We promote these singular individuals as Kresge Eminent Artists not because they need us. We promote them because we, the community of metro Detroit, want to very publicly acknowledge that we need them.

To elevate our Eminent Artists is to signal far and wide that Detroit is a community that embraces its artists. That embrace of our Eminent Artists goes hand in hand with the support that our partners at Kresge Arts in Detroit provide to artists, ranging from the early-career risk takers who earn Gilda Awards to the professional artists throughout their careers who receive Kresge Artist Fellowships.

Our 300 Gilda Awardees and Fellows have collectively received $6.6 million in support. After their awards, we watch as they continue on to further career heights and additional awards validating the wisdom of their selection.

One of those additional awards recently went to a 2011 Kresge Artist Fellow by the name of Olayami Dabls. He is the first Fellow to become an Eminent Artist. I'm sure he won't be the last.

This monograph captures his amazing tale of struggle, self-discovery and slow realization of enormous talent. It is the tale of the mark that talent, in turn, has made on this city.

Like all of his Eminent Artist predecessors, he has mightily contributed to our artistic and cultural landscape. Like the late muralist Charles McGee and the Detroit Opera House visionary David DiChiera, he has unmistakably altered our physical landscape as well.

In his grandest work, he has reimagined a set of abandoned buildings and debris-strewn fields as a vibrant campus and sculpture garden to tell a story of throwing off mental chains of colonialism to celebrate African roots. It is an exciting story for our times, still in progress, a story that Olayami Dabls quite literally invites us all to enter.

RIP RAPSON

PRESIDENT AND CEO
THE KRESGE FOUNDATION

"PEOPLE MAKE THE MISTAKE OF THINKING I'M AN ARTIST"

ARTIST STATEMENT

"If you say you're an artist, then there's a perimeter which you're working in. If you're a storyteller, that means there has to be some relevance to whatever you're doing. What I am doing is having fun with history, communicating specific information to my culture group that anyone can enjoy. I make statements that are perceived as art when it's really just the tools I use. In early African communities, art always had a clear definition: If it doesn't serve a purpose for the community, it was discarded. I'm telling a story for the community and for myself."

OLAYAMI DABLS, 2022

OF MYTH AND MEANING

How Olayami Dabls transformed himself and a desolate Detroit street corner into global symbols of African culture and artistic excellence

NICHoLE M. CHRISTIAN

It is the storyteller who makes us who we are, who creates history.
The storyteller creates the memory that the survivors must
have — otherwise their surviving would have no meaning.
CHINUA ACHEBE

f Olayami Dabls had his way, this story, his story, would open and close near the corner of Grand River Avenue and West Grand Boulevard in Detroit. Perhaps it would be mostly silent to match his belief that images have power beyond words.

"Where you have symbols, you don't necessarily need a lot of words. You let people come and figure out what they need to know," he says. "If there's any meaning, they'll get it."

Much like the murals that have transformed this once nondescript intersection, Olayami Dabls is a mystifying character. What there is to know about his life and how he has navigated his 73 years is neither neat nor easily gleaned. Yet the essence, he insists, lives and breathes on this corner: the path he took to become simply *Dabls*, the way he views the world, and how he's helped reshape a corner of it.

Most eyes agree: This is no common street intersection. One does not simply drive by. Untamed and unending creativity live here. You draw closer because that's what the cluster of buildings, former row houses and adjacent outdoor installations demand of everyone. These are canvases come-to-life: illuminated by jarring colors and repurposed scraps of wood, iron and glass that have been glued and nailed and aligned with intent. Every dot, every line, every circle set free to grab your gaze. And you will most assuredly look and see yourself looking, into the mirror, multiples of them. Mirrors, partial slabs and jagged slivers affixed like

Nkisi House as seen from Grand River Avenue, and (inset) in its previous incarnation.

PREVIOUS PAGES Detail from the mural *Honor The African Woman Who Has Endured Colonization And Enslavement* in the Eastern Market district.

scattered puzzle pieces onto every structure. This, too, is by design: Dabls wishes you to see yourself in this place. That the mirrors are broken and cracked is purposeful too: Dabls' playful rebuke of the ancient Romans' lore claiming broken mirrors transmit seven years of bad luck.

Here, the broken mirrors reflect only beauty, and in vivid hues of blue, red, yellow, orange and white. Meticulously aligned dots, lines and ancient African symbols cover virtually every door, window and wall. "There's nothing on this campus that's here just for the purpose of aesthetics. The dots represent the children," he explains during a guided tour. "The mirrors are the portals. The lines are male and female energy, vertical and horizontal together, but feminine energy is the most powerful on the planet."

On sunny days, the shards of mirrors and bursts of colors treat observant eyes to a kaleidoscopic dance as the light somehow finds new ways to illuminate the wonder that is here. But explosive color is only the tip of the tale of how this intersection, once a patch of urban desolation, was transformed into an unapologetically Black — African to be exact — beacon of history and artistic excellence.

"It was designed just to get people who were driving down Grand River to look," Dabls explains. "But I made sure that everything I put up had a meaning for being here. I couldn't do art just for art's sake."

Art's elite and Hollywood stars such as actor Wesley Snipes and filmmaker Quentin Tarantino have made pilgrimages to see what makes Grand River and Grand Boulevard stand out in Detroit's ongoing phoenix tale; and why it may even be rightly looked upon as one of the most authentic embodiments of the city's motto, *Speramus meliora; resurget cineribus*. "We hope for better things; it will rise from the ashes."

If there is energy on this corner, it has come through Dabls' hands, his paint brushes, and a slow evolving vision for the once-bland brick buildings and trash-strewn lots collectively known as the MBAD African Bead Museum. While it is often referred to simply as "the Bead Museum," the space is a full block-long campus of accessible outdoor installations and murals covering buildings that are largely inaccessible, save for the small retail shop where Dabls sells beads.

Internet photos of the museum's campus and its maze-like sculpture garden featuring 18 installations, such as *Iron Teaching Rocks How to Rust*, *Nkisi House* and *African Scripted Language Wall*, continue to lead camera-wielding tourists to the corner. They come in droves, many of them white. In warm months, visitors join Dabls on the stoop outside of the retail shop or walk the installations beside him as he rewinds back to MBAD's beginning and recounts its cultural meaning.

THE CULTURE KEEPER

The south side of MBAD and the signature symbols and sign are familiar sights to Detroiters driving along the nearby I-96 freeway.

"When I came here in 1998, people thought I was out of my mind," recalls Dabls. "It was like wilderness, a complete dumping ground. There was debris and trash everywhere. No windows or doors. I had a few ideas about curb appeal, but they didn't have anything to do with what this place has become. It's really beyond my wildest imagination."

The fashion magazine *Elle* deemed MBAD's campus artful enough for a full spread featuring haute models parading and posing all along Grand River at the intersection of Grand Boulevard. The scene, one of many over the years, speaks to an evolution that Dabls never anticipated. Another example of that evolution: A $100,000 crowdfunding campaign in late 2018 helped open the museum's first public gallery (although the COVID-19 pandemic forced Dabls to halt activities). Architect Lorcan O'Herlihy, noted for his work on the Louvre Museum in Paris, donated his time, and that of his firm LOHA, for the design.

Dabls sits, as he has each day for years, with his glasses high on his forehead and his body perched atop a stool behind the counter in the museum campus retail shop. Surrounded by strands of dangling and intentionally unlabeled beads, he tells the story of his collection and of the struggles he's endured including lacking the resources to open the actual museum building, the corner structure facing Grand River and Grand Boulevard.

AFRICAN SCRIPTED LANGUAGE WALL

NKISI HOUSE

EMPTY APARTMENT
BUILDING WITH
COLLAPSED ROOF

IRON TEACHING ROCKS
HOW TO RUST

GRAND RIVER AVE

VINEWOOD ST

THREE SMALL TOWNHOMES
CURRENTLY HOUSING THE BEAD
GALLERY, DABLS' STUDIO, AND
THE AFRICAN ART COLLECTION

ABOVE An aerial photograph of the MBAD Bead Museum campus.
OPPOSITE The collapsed interior of the museum's main corner building.

To the public, it is indistinguishable from the other mural-covered buildings
that have been wrapped with symmetrical symbols, mirrors and vivid colors. But
it is only a shell. The roof is gone. So are all traces of an interior. It is a ruin and a
roadblock to the MBAD African Bead Museum's future. Only mural-covered brick
walls and the hope of a full renovation remain. A large, weather-damaged skylight
window collapsed in 2006 and sent the building's roof and second floor plunging
into the basement.

To see the scale of the rubble — piles of wood and dangling cords, surrounded
by crumpled books, rusty file cabinets and stacks of dust-covered art works — is to
understand, and yet legitimately question, Dabls' insistence on his dream. The
dream persists, he says, because he does. "This place and me is almost one," he
says guiding a rare tour inside. "When something is the only thing you're doing,

you have to keep going. I never had the option to stop believing or to say I'm out of business. I can still see the vision."

One day the doors will open, he vows, and the ruin will have been transformed into the home for a treasure trove of artifacts, masks, statues, textiles and other art pieces he's kept stored away for years. "I wasn't gonna let myself self-defeat and just sell the stuff."

This is a man stirred by steady steps and cosmic imagination. "I've noticed that when I work with what I have, it brings what I need into existence, into the universe. The brain has the ear first. Therefore, it [opening of the main building] will manifest, if it's going to."

Unfettered imagination and singular creative vision are precisely what has turned Olayami Dabls, and the corner he's cultivated for nearly 25 years, into a distinct Detroit attraction. Some say a legacy of bold cultural expression more than justifies Dabls' selection as the 14th recipient of Detroit's most prestigious arts honor, the Kresge Eminent Artist Award.

"He's way past being just an artist," says Efe Bess, a celebrated local African drummer who met Dabls in the late 1980s. "An artist is a person who's creating for other people's approval," says Bess who, like Dabls, exchanged his given name for an African one. "Dabls sees in terms of culture not only color. He's someone who's tapped back into his DNA," explains Bess, an inaugural member of MBAD's board. "We're lucky that he had the visions to want to share it the way that he has."

The 13 Kresge Eminent Artists who precede Dabls are among Detroit's most pioneering and masterful creatives. The group is comprised of the late painter and sculptor Charles McGee; the late jazz trumpeter Marcus Belgrave; poet and playwright Bill Harris; the late poet and publisher Naomi Long Madgett; the late composer and Michigan Opera Theatre Artistic Director David DiChiera; the late photographer Bill Rauhauser; textile designer Ruth Adler Schnee; photographer and activist Leni Sinclair; harpist and educator Patricia Terry-Ross; jazz saxophonist Wendell Harrison; poet, educator and activist Gloria House; ceramicist Marie Woo; and painter, art educator and historian Shirley Woodson.

"Each of our Kresge Eminent Artists has contributed mightily to our artistic and cultural landscape, but Olayami Dabls is one of those whose work has altered our physical landscape as well," said The Kresge Foundation's President Rip Rapson. "The mirrored and multicolored Dabls MBAD African Bead Museum and its adjoining sculpture garden shout to passersby that the human spirit is alive and dynamic near the intersection of Grand River and Grand Boulevard on Detroit's west side. Both in that monumental work and thousands of smaller ones,

THE CULTURE KEEPER

A detail of the mural *Trade Beads and Snakes* on Grand River Avenue.

Dabls connects all of us to the story of African Americans and African roots while looking boldly to the future."

Dabls' entrance into this illustrious group comes with added distinction. He is the first Kresge Eminent Artist to have won a Kresge Artist Fellowship (2011), the $25,000 no-strings-attached award given annually to 20 metro Detroit artists across various disciplines. Beyond the creation of the museum is a body of artistic achievement spanning a half-century in Detroit, which includes, he estimates, more than 15,000 original pieces of art — paintings, murals, installations and sculptures and jewelry.

When the news of his selection as the 2022 Kresge Eminent Artist first reached him, Dabls was blunt. "I'm excited about the money," he said, referring to the award's unrestricted $50,000 purse.

However, in the weeks after his selection and the flurry of attention and publicity it brought, Dabls' perspective began to change. It even prompted him to review years of photos on his public Flickr account to track MBAD's transformation.

"This tells me that what I came up with works, that you can have these two city blocks and murals — here on Grand River and at the Eastern Market — that are immersed in African material culture, and people who may not even understand it still will connect with what you're doing," he says.

He adds: "I guess it says I'm doing something right." The consensus is a resounding yes.

"You can't look at Dabls' work and not see Detroit, a city that's sometimes fragmented, but it's a work of beauty at the same time," explains Dan Carmody, president of Detroit's Eastern Market, 43 acres of eateries, bars, retail businesses, meat packing plants and more wrapped around a six-block open-air produce market that dates to 1891. And in recent years, a program called Murals in the Market has commissioned scores of murals, giving locals and tourists another reason to flock there. Among the murals are two created by Dabls: *Honor the African Woman Who Has Endured Colonization and Enslavement* and *Sankofa*.

THE CULTURE KEEPER

ABOVE The mural *Honor The African Woman Who Has Endured Colonization And Enslavement* in the Eastern Market district of Detroit.

FOLLOWING PAGES a detail from the mural *Trade Beads and Snakes* on Grand River Avenue.

"With Dabls, the colors and designs are impressive," Carmody says, "but there are important stories in his work that give context and history to a city that's 80% African American." Both of Dabls' market murals feature some of the reoccurring symbols that make his work unmistakably African inspired, including the mythical Sankofa bird of Ghana, which is always depicted with its feet planted forward and its head in the opposite direction as an homage to Akan people's belief that: *It is not taboo to go back and fetch what you forgot.*

Carmody calls Dabls one of Detroit's finest public artists: "You know that you're looking at his work even if you don't know everything he's communicating."

To Satori Shakoor, Dabls' artistry is about more than medium mastery. She sees him as a vital link in the chain of creative movements that enliven Detroit. "He's

25

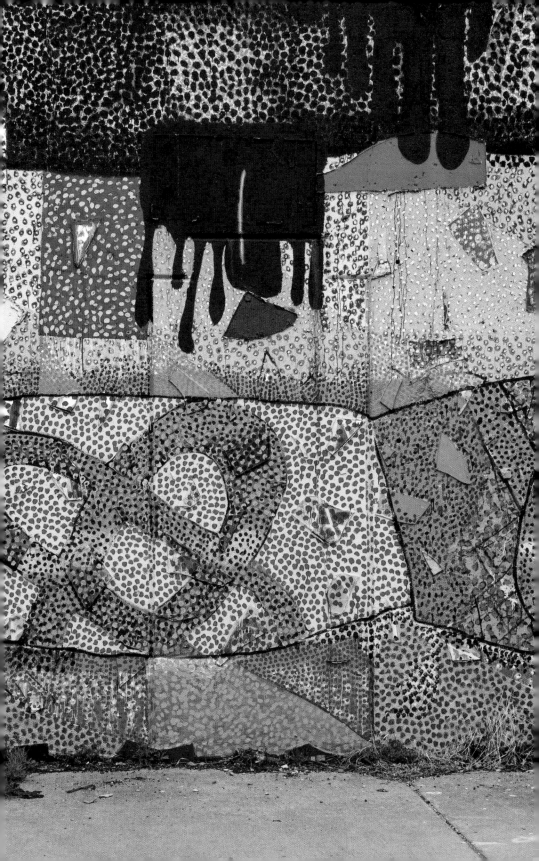

drawn the whole world to a corner, that's this amazing backdrop, a mirror really, of the energy of the people who live here."

Shakoor was among the five panelists charged with choosing the 2022 Kresge Eminent Artist. She speaks about Dabls with artist-to-artist admiration. Her work as founder of "The Secret Society of Twisted Storytellers," an award-winning live storytelling show, has taught her how to observe stories closely. Olayami Dabls, she says, has lived one filled with chapters that exemplify the spirit of the Eminent Artist award.

"It's not just about the art that you produce but about what you're leaving, who you are as a human in the city, what you represent and how you interact through your art with the community," says Shakoor, who is also host of "Detroit Performs," a local public television arts and culture show. "This is someone who checks and connects all the boxes."

Long before she was a panelist, Shakoor was just another passerby struck by "brilliance just out there on the corner." While her grandkids would ooh and ahh from the backseat as she drove by the museum, Shakoor always found herself transported to another creative era in Detroit—that of Motown Records, the homegrown pathbreaking music company launched in 1959. Founder Berry Gordy had a penchant for plucking up-and-coming performers from the neighborhoods, where many of them continued to live even as their fame was rising. Singers Smokey Robinson, Martha Reeves and members of the legendary groups The Temptations and Four Tops were among them.

"I think of it like the city in the '60s when all the superstars, everybody was embedded in the community. Everybody could inspire everybody even if you were just on the street corner applauding the guys who just got out of Ford Motors and Chrysler with their dreams of a Berry Gordy offer."

Shakoor sums up the 2022 selection with pride: "Mr. Dabls is Detroit."

Origins Undone

Ask Olayami Dabls about his African Bead Museum, African material culture or philosophy in general and he flips effortlessly through epochs. He is a man at home in ancient times. You know it by the ease in his voice, the steely glint that comes over his eyes.

Yet not all history is equal. Some passages of are off limits: Chapter 1 of Dabls' life, the first 18 years.

Dabls is uninterested in connecting the dots and dates of his life in neat obedience to the curiosity of others. "Everything," he says, "is not for consumption."

Dabls' childhood home, painted from memory in 1981 when he was known as James Lewis.

Dabls is a careful curator of the tales of his formative years, the life he lived on the way to becoming Dabls. "The story of what's been done is more important than how I got here to this point," he explains. By choice, his parents are unnamed. A younger sister is mentioned but shrouded in mystery too.

The details that are shared are offered in pieces. "I came to Detroit on a train with a shoebox full of chicken," he recalls. "I think I got off at Michigan Central or someplace. Looked up and I was here."

For reasons unexplained, Dabls rolled into Detroit as a "runaway." At the time, he was only "about 10 or 11" but tall and determined enough to decide for himself that it was time to outrun the life circumstances that accompanied his birth, as James Arthur Lewis in October of 1948, in Canton, Mississippi.

Life in the heat and hatred of the segregated Jim Crow South gave young James little to be encouraged about, and no early evidence of Picasso's famous claim that "every child is an artist." In fact, James Lewis' first-known attempt at art would not come until age 18, in Detroit, when a nagging fascination with the solar system led him to create a "crude" painting of the planets as they existed in his imagination. A later acrylic painting of a 1948 Southern shack serves as somewhat of a family photo. The painting is what Dabls remembers of the house where he was born. No people are present.

His reflections are matter of fact, stripped of any sense of nostalgia. "Most Black boys in the South back then didn't have a childhood," he says. "Only thing I was gonna do was be a day laborer, do some manual work, or stay at home, let Daddy kick my ass, make me learn the verses, and go to church. Somehow, I knew I could do better. People told me I was mature."

Why Dabls chose Detroit is unclear and, he maintains, unimportant.

"I don't think I've even heard the whole story," says Dabls daughter, 35-year-old Alake Williams, who is the youngest of Dabls' four children. "He's never been one to really talk about or dwell on his life. He really is quiet about some things," says Williams, who owns and operates Olive Mode, a women's fashion boutique in one of the smaller buildings on the MBAD campus site.

One figure from his early childhood — an uncle — is mentioned repeatedly, albeit briefly. The facts, as Dabls shares them, are few. At some point, the uncle moved to Flint, Michigan. "They said he was an artist," Dabls recalls. "That rung a bell with me, 'Oh, maybe that's what I want to be.' But you know, in the South, in fact, there wasn't too many places in the North you could do that unless you had family in one of the good jobs, education, working for the government or whatever."

Whether the uncle ("I couldn't tell you what his name was") or whether anyone else was awaiting young James' arrival is left unanswered. So, too, are the broader questions of how a young boy with little more than a third-grade education decided to flee his home for Motown and the hope of a world unknown.

"I ran away because I didn't like what they wanted me to do," he says. "I knew I had rights."

Looking back, he says, "My brain was way ahead of my age and all of that begins to make sense when you realize you've got 200,000 years of information inside you that just needs to be triggered." Though he's only 73 years old, Dabls is insistent that every living being carries a more ancient and inexplicable reservoir of innate cultural knowledge. "I knew I would make the right decisions to get me to where I am."

Dabls says the sharper details and other open questions — who did he live with? how did he, as a child, support himself? — have become irrelevant and too distant to be of value to him. "Nobody was really caring about those kinds of things," he explains. "I have always been tall, so, therefore, I could get a job. No one wanted to know how old I was. They wanted to know if I could do the work."

For a time, home was near what was then considered Detroit's North End neighborhood — Gladstone and 12th streets. "It was a unique experience," he recalls with an open grin. Around age 19, a woman named Barbara caught Dabls'

Dabls in his early twenties in Detroit.

attention. She was 10 years older. "I think that tells you something about my mentality," he says erupting into a laugh.

Barbara owned a red 1965 Ford Mustang which thrilled him. He'd met her younger brothers hanging around a neighborhood pool hall. "They adopted me." The brothers, all seven, also frightened him though not enough to douse the spark he felt for Barbara. They married two years later, determined to settle down in a neighborhood teeming with dreamers and hustlers to the beat of the Motown sound raging in the streets and all across the country. "Everybody was trying to imitate the Motown musicians, or they wanted to be pimps or pool hustlers, unless you had family and they worked in the factory, and they insisted you go to school, or you just did something else."

In Dabls' case, that "something else" was the Vietnam War. He was drafted in 1968 and set to become, by the war's end, one of the estimated 300,000 African Americans who served. "It was a true Wild, Wild West over there. For the first time on the planet, Black men had some power. It's another story that's never really been told from the point of view of Black people. It changed my life being over there."

Dabls' stint ironically required a brief return to the South to train with the U. S. Army, first at Ft. Knox in Kentucky and then to Ft. Polk, a base in Vernon Parish, Louisiana. He struggled to find ease using a gun. "The gun is made for right-handed people so when the cartridge ejects you don't see it with your eyes. It goes to the left," he says. "I'm left-handed and I shoot left-handed. I couldn't really get past seeing the cartridge eject to the left, too," he said explaining his fear of being struck in the eye each time the bullet cartridge released.

Eventually, he was deployed to Da Nang, site of the largest U.S. airbase in what was then South Vietnam. A small stroke of luck spared him from combat. "If you're the only son in a family, the government had a rule to not put you in the infantry," Dabls explained. He worked in the base retail store throughout his time in the service. "I never had to use my gun. People thought I was special."

Indeed, Da Nang propelled Dabls. "I learned to read and write," he says. "It gave me a voice. I had been faking being literate. You can easily do that; you just mimic the language around you. Nobody's gonna ever ask you, 'You go to school, boy?' They make the assumption that you did."

The Army was his gateway to a General Equivalency Diploma, a milestone for a young man who'd left the South having completed "maybe the third grade" and holding scant hope of ever carrying his education further. "Before I began to study, I was depressed thinking I'm a failure because I don't know grammar and spelling. I had a teacher helping me, the colonel's wife. One day, she said to him, in front of everybody, 'This guy here, he's gonna go places.'"

This is a piece of the past welcomed by Dabls. He smiles, slows his words as he travels back. "I think my brain knew she was right," he says. "I just had to catch up to the knowledge. Looks like I did. I guess."

Culture Calls

By the time Dabls, who was still James Lewis, was discharged from the Army in 1970, he'd become an exuberant student of life, thirsty for knowledge and opportunity.

He was also about to become a family man. Barbara was pregnant with a baby girl named Davida, his first child, born in 1971. Soon after Davida's birth, Barbara, who was a graduate of Wayne State University and "the computer person for a company in Detroit," planted a seed.

She said, "Are you gonna go to school to get you some more education?" Dabls recalls. "The way she said it changed something."

In the end, Barbara ignited an important life change. "I never identified myself as being in that elitist group of wanting or being able to go to school. But it was like she was telling me that I could, and I had the GI Bill. So, hell, I believed."

FOLLOWING PAGES A view of *Wood Reservation*, part of the permanent outdoor installation at the museum.

Dabls on duty in Da Nang during the Vietnam War.

Dabls enrolled at Highland Park Community College. "Of all the classes that they had, drafting seemed like the only one that didn't require a lot of reading and writing so I took that."

The college had opened in 1918 as an outgrowth of Henry Ford's decision to grow the size of his automotive production line in Highland Park, only a few miles north of the Piquette Avenue Plant in Detroit, home of the Model T assembly line. The Highland Park of the early 1900s was the place where Ford's vision of a world on wheels revved into high gear. Lured by the promise of a $5 per day wage, workers descended on what was then a modest village. Between 1910 and 1920, the population increased by 1,000% and became a catalyst for the college's creation.

James Lewis (r) and a friend, while at Fort Knox.

Dabls' arrival on campus coincided with major demographic shifts in Highland Park, as white working-class families continued to take advantage of growth in freeways and the resulting urban sprawl. More than half of the once white college students were now Black; like Dabls, many were returning veterans eager to take advantage of the GI Bill to pay for their education.

Just as the Army had been a pivotal proving ground, Highland Park Community College also had much to teach Dabls. "My first encounter or contact with culture other than Western culture was at Highland Park Community College," he says. "Back then, it was a college that emphasized a connection with Africa. There was literature that was based on African writers and scholars. There was a whole floor that had African murals on the walls, which was unique in and of itself."

Decades passed before he realized how central the college was on his burgeoning journey of self-discovery. Years later he enrolled as a part-time student at Wayne State University to study mechanical engineering and art but "drifted away" due to the pressure of family life, full-time work, and a lingering sense of doubt about his path. "Being at Wayne was too much," he says.

Wayne didn't offer the learning environment he'd fallen in love with during his early 20s at Highland Park Community College. Though he'd enrolled intent on majoring in drafting and minoring in art, Dabls devoured every guest lecture, particularly those with emphasis on history and culture. "The place really got my

TOP LEFT Dabls with civil rights icon Rosa Parks (left) and wife S. Jill Miller (center).
BOTTOM LEFT S. Jill Miller and Dabls at their wedding in Detroit.
RIGHT Dabls with three of his four children (top to bottom) Bakari,
Makeda, and Alake.

attention," he says. "Here I was, all of a sudden, thinking I was '*the it*' when really I didn't know *shit* about the self or my own particular culture group. They were hitting me with all this information that could be substantiated or backed up."

Highland Park Community College closed in 1995, after Michigan's governor at the time, John Engler, stripped the school from the state's budget priorities due to reported "chronic" financial failure. However, in Dabls' memory, the college remains a place of intellectual transformation. "It's where I got thrown into myself," Dabls says. "The teachers, the art, it really set up a hell of a conflict in me about what it meant to learn for yourself versus just assimilating."

The strength of the college's drafting program pushed Dabls into his first professional job. While finishing up his associate's degree in drafting technology, he was hired as an apprentice in an automotive drafting program for General Motors' Chevrolet division. The office was based at the sprawling GM Tech Center, in Warren, once a notoriously unwelcoming all-white working-class border suburb northeast of Detroit.

An early self-portrait, made in pencil.

The pay was great. The office environment was not. "I hated General Motors," he says.

Dabls landed the job as part of the division's "first affirmative action group, meaning Black folks and white women," he says. Though he was only a few miles from the Detroit city line, the world felt foreign. "It was a complete immersion into a culture that was entirely different from the city." In Warren, he was surrounded by 500 mostly white co-workers. The dominant shirt and tie style became his style too. He also gave his weekends to staff softball. "I could hit a ball 300 feet away."

But Dabls refused two things: Office golf outings ("You gotta have some money to buy all that equipment and have it sitting in the closet 'til the next weekend") and finding humor in endless jokes about then-Detroit Mayor Coleman A. Young. In 1974, Young swept into history as Motown's first Black mayor, a position he would hold for a record 20 years. He brought with him history-making military credentials, having served as a World War II bombardier with the Tuskegee Airmen, the first Black pilot unit in the U.S. military.

More notable for some, though, was Young's fondness for the f-bomb and other salty, in-your-face forms of speech. "Swearing," he famously said, "is an art form. You can express yourself much more directly, much more exactly, much more succinctly, with properly used curse words."

A widespread dislike for Young greeted Dabls daily. "I'd have to sit up out there as they bashed Coleman Young every day. Seemed like every person in that room

Dabls with two of the many paintings he created during his time as curator and artist-in-residence at Detroit's Afro-American Museum, the precursor to the Charles H. Wright Museum.

had some complaint about Detroit. It was mindboggling to me because the only thing they knew about Detroit was Coleman and that he cussed too much to be a mayor. They'd tell you how they never even been to Detroit."

Most days, Dabls went to work with the urge to quit knotted in his throat. But adult responsibilities were staring at him too. "GM was paying the bills, so I couldn't do nothing too foolish, nothing but go to work every day and pretend like I liked it."

Dabls punctuates the nearly 50-year-old memory with humor. "I don't know how I got out of Warren alive," he jokes. "For some reason, they allowed me to live."

Though known to be primarily a quiet reclusive man, Dabls has an edgy, well-timed wit and he's as precise with it as he is with his paint brush or pencil.

"I don't want people to take me so seriously," he says. "We got too many serious people on the planet as it is. It's good to laugh." And when the laughs come, he's often first, and freely, laughing at himself.

Humor is also a part of how Dabls retells the incident that almost took his life in 1975. On his way to work one morning, "a car rear-ended me and just changed everything. I think the universe knew I didn't belong in no white shirt, white pants, white shoes, out there playing golf and softball, trying to fit in."

Instead, for nearly three years, Dabls was in and out of hospitals, plagued by piercing back pains. He struggled to sit, to sleep, to stand, to walk. "I think I must've been in every hospital in Detroit; one of them I was in for nine months."

Along the way, depression surfaced. Dabls, who was in his late 20s, started therapy. "Black people don't tend to have the time or money stacked up to just transition to another career," he says. "But I'm a firm believer that if you put your brain to work, it will find a way to transition you to whatever you want to do. Sometimes it can be painful as hell, but my brain and my body knew I had to get out of there."

When he disclosed that he'd begun making art only a few years earlier at age 18, his psychologist suggested he give more attention to his painting and drawing to help combat his stress. In the suggestion was a clue toward a career turning point. In hindsight, he says, "I was being prepared for everything I'm doing now."

A Right Next Move

Dr. Charles Howard Wright and Olayami Dabls emerged from different eras of the same segregated South.

Wright, born in 1918 in Alabama, was a prominent Black obstetrician and gynecologist, a graduate of Meharry Medical College, a legendary historically Black college in Nashville, Tennessee. Meharry opened a decade after the end of the Civil War with a mighty mission to ensure Black Americans had access to Black doctors and medical workers.

In 1946, three years after graduating, and two years before Dabls was born, Wright made his way to Detroit. Here, he began a thriving medical career. He would also dedicate a portion of his office on West Grand Boulevard to a new museum for the preservation of African American history.

Wright hatched the idea for the museum after seeing a monument to World War II soldiers in Denmark. Wright and the 36 others who backed the idea and the 1965 museum launch decided it needed an expansive name to go along with the mission. Their goal was to celebrate the lives of notable Black Detroiters and to showcase artifacts that Wright had collected during his travels, including African masks from Ghana and Nigeria. They chose The International Afro-American

Board, staff and other supporters photographed in front of the first home of the International Afro-American Museum in 1981. See following pages for IDs.

Museum. It was the precursor to the Charles H. Wright Museum of African American History, now one of the largest cultural institutions of its kind in the nation.

Yet the museum that helped define Dabls started with a smaller vision. He recalls the Wright first as a fast-moving rumor among Black artists who were hungry for a welcoming space to exhibit. Black artists wanted a counterpoint to the local galleries that were primarily white and off limits. Membership flyers were floating around the city urging Black families and professionals to join the new museum and to tell others. At time, Dabls was still working at GM, which gave him an idea. "Every Black person on the job, I strong-armed them into taking out a membership," he said laughing. "It wasn't hard; it was the '70s. Black people were starting to ask questions and feel pride."

As an excuse to visit, Dabls hand-delivered a batch of new member cards but was dumbstruck by the things he did not see: a staff and signs of life on the walls. "I thought the museum was this major operation that was in full gear," he says. "I got over there, and I realized that what I was promoting and advertising on the job was just mainly in my head," he explained. "The museum part of it didn't exist yet. It was just three row houses with an office, boxes and nothing happening."

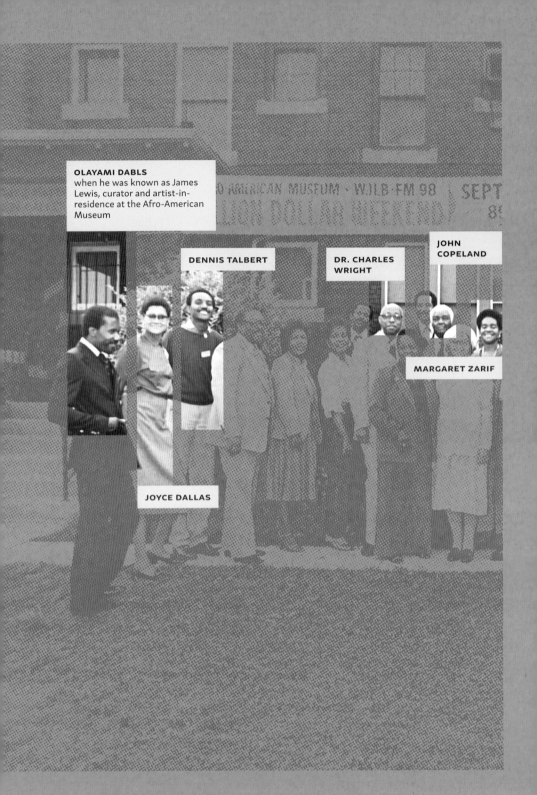

OLAYAMI DABLS
when he was known as James Lewis, curator and artist-in-residence at the Afro-American Museum

DENNIS TALBERT

DR. CHARLES WRIGHT

JOHN COPELAND

MARGARET ZARIF

JOYCE DALLAS

42

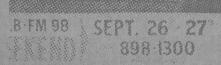

.B·FM 98
EREND

SEPT. 26 · 27
898·1300

ROBERT SHANNON

ROSA PARKS

BILLIE VANLEER

EULA McCLANEY

S. JILL MILLER
volunteer and
Dabls' future wife

MARK C. SMITH

43

After the accident, when he shared this experience during a therapy session, his psychologist, who was also Black, pushed him to get more engaged. At this point in his life, working for long periods was unbearable. Art provided solace. Paintings and drawings began to pile up right along with a mounting sense of boredom and isolation. At the psychologist's suggestion, he decided to turn the surplus of time and art into something more. From his visit, he knew that the museum needed both. Within months, Dabls was creating art for its walls and displays. Eventually, he wound his way into a position as the curator and artist-in-residence.

"Wright had the building; he had the money, but he couldn't be there on a day-to-day basis because he was out there delivering babies. Everyone else had 9-to-5's too," he said. "I got all kinds of stuff tossed at me." Dabls' ability to adapt and, some say, innovate, kept him on staff at the museum for 15 years through several membership and fundraising drives, and two expansions.

One of the museum's major goals during his time was to broaden awareness of the American Civil Rights Movement. For a tiny new museum with a thin budget, this was a massive undertaking. "The Civil Rights Decade" was intended to collapse two decades of history visually and thematically. "I needed pictures." The costs of acquiring the rights to display original photos were too high to even consider. So Dabls stopped asking.

The exhibit featured nearly 90 cutouts incorporating a mix of felt designs, painting, and drawing. "They were a quicker and affordable way of doing something that could be readily displayed and moved around as art but also used for people to get an idea of the decade."

Dabls made the series slowly, each cutout crafted as an element of the movement; they were faceless figures, Black and white, young and old, dramatizing pivotal moments in America's civil rights struggle. The Montgomery bus boycott, Dr. Martin Luther King Jr.'s assassination and infamous school desegregation cases were among the primary subjects for the series. He transformed each subject, effectively muting some of the terror and trauma embedded in the history by using a palette of colors that would appeal as much to adult members as to the young children who'd visit on school field trips.

The exhibition also traveled around metro Detroit by request, with stops at public schools, city, county and federal buildings, and a 2017 re-creation was displayed

OPPOSITE *Dr. M. L. King's Vision*, collage with pastel and chalk on paper, 11x14". From the 1985 series "The Civil Rights Decade."

FOLLOWING PAGES *James Meredith*, collage with pastel and chalk on paper, 11x14", from "The Civil Rights Decade."

36
JAMES MEREDITH
12-9-1985
J. LEWIS

Caption text within the image:

From a 1982 *Ebony* article about Detroit's Afro American Museum and the rise of others like it in America.

in the lobby of Detroit's ornate Fisher Building (many of the original cutouts were lost in the Bead Museum's roof collapse).

The Fisher is where Bryce Detroit, an Afrofuturist storyteller, and an award-winning music recording artist and producer, saw the series and its impact. Though it was only a re-creation of the original, it is etched in Bryce's memory. He points to it as evidence of why he views Dabls as "a living icon," whom he credits as a force in his embrace of a more African identity.

"His knowledge of African material culture takes the cake," he says, "But then to see the cutouts, man; it's just so clear this is a dude operating at a whole different level; he's his own-ass universe. The mastery of form, the mastery of shapes, cultural symbols, and the mastery of geometry; he's using it all, telling an entire history, an entire legacy just from some pieces of cardboard."

Bryce saw several of Dabls' original sketches and art pieces back in 2011, after a friend invited him to tag along to help an "elder" artist do some work on a wall. The wall would turn out to be one of the museum's key installations, the *African Scripted Language Wall*. But for Bryce the revelation that day was seeing the work Dabls had locked away, all created under the name James Lewis.

"In real, real life he could've stayed James and become like a Romare Bearden," Bryce says, referring to a painter and collagist regarded as one of the most important African American artists. Bryce stands by the comparison. For him, Dabls "is a straight-up real fine artist in *real* life. The fact that he doesn't in any way identify with that work is hilarious. It's so bossy, so baller."

Dabls discussing history with Detroit schoolchildren at the former Cornerstone School.

To this day, Dabls regards the cutout series as a seminal foreshadowing of his shift from artist to visual storyteller. "I'd always worked in series," he says, "but unbeknownst to me, I was using my art to tell stories about our past, not realizing that was an ancient way of disseminating information to your culture group. That's exactly what I'm doing today; I just understand it now."

Watching adults' reactions to the cutouts was unexpectedly revealing. He realized many "had lived through most of what I was communicating. I was just triggering memories; that's what made it powerful, the story, not the tool I was using."

In 2018, Dabls resurrected a portion of the "The Civil Rights Decade" for an illustrated self-published book, *The Story of Our Rights: How a Nation Moved Toward Social Justice*. The illustrations, a halting mix of lush colors and faceless silhouettes, are as evocative as the original cutouts.

"There were African people who rejected the notion of marching, turning the other cheek, and working with their former oppressor to be included in a so-called civil rights movement," he writes in the book's foreword. "There are those today who still question the Civil Rights Movement, arguing that they became rights with no substance. Africans are a complex people, and no one idea will get the attention of all."

This is an understanding Dabls arrived at slowly after decades of questioning, intense study, self-observation and finally reimagining his relationship to culture, identity and creative expression. "I was trying to figure out some things about myself," he explains. "And doing it in the '70s, you're talking about a time when the idea of African and African American history was looked upon as a joke."

49

ABOVE *Freedom Schools*, collage with pastel and chalk on paper, 11x14". From the series "The Civil Rights Decade."

OPPOSITE *Terror*, collage with pastel and chalk on paper, 11x14". From the series "The Civil Rights Decade."

Nevertheless, Dabls continued to pore over books about ancient African civilizations because the museum was beginning a collection for research. Part of his job was choosing what to purchase and then sharing his knowledge as he led museum tours. As the books piled up, so did Dabls' internal conflicts.

"I had the European concept about what art is: It's something you create to sell to generate revenue. I had been miseducated about my own culture group. I started to think, you could spend your whole life with a miseducation and do pretty good. It's not an issue unless you're thinking or contemplating what you're doing and who you are on the planet," he said.

Meanwhile, he took it upon himself to incorporate more of the expressly African objects such as masks and statues of deities in the expanding collection. Museum visits were growing, yet an unstated discomfort was in the air. Some of it was between him and Wright and almost always conveyed second or third hand. "It was a love-hate relationship," Dabls says. "He wanted exhibits. But some of the exhibits that I had he didn't always like."

Dabls recalls a collection of carvings that had been donated to the museum. "We had to take them off display because people were afraid of them. I was trying to figure out why are Black people afraid of these pieces; they're just our great-great-great-great grandparents communicating. But it's hard to use logic to overcome fear. Most people still don't realize how Western culture teaches us to fear Africa."

However, Dabls' growing interest in centering what he called ancestral African art and the museum's desire to grow its audience and its offerings eventually aligned in 1983 as the museum decided to bring an annual festival of the African diaspora to Hart Plaza on Detroit's waterfront.

The festival gave Dabls his first real-world connection with Africa outside of books and the classroom. Much of what he'd read about African material culture was now spread before him: masks, carvings, textiles, symbols, metals, jewelry and tons of beads. "The museum gave me a very good working knowledge of what people of African descent had done in this country," he explained. "But when the museum started doing the festivals, I was exposed to Africans and actual material culture. They knew the meaning and they taught me."

Dabls the student of African culture became an instant private collector, particularly of beads. "The beads became the conduit for me to do what I always wanted to do with culture," he says.

The popularity of the African World Festival soared; it continues today. But Dabls and Wright's museum had different destinies. In fact, at the height of the museum's drive for further expansion, Dabls resigned.

Just as he'd done as a young boy, he sensed a truer, freer future elsewhere.

LEFT Dabls at the Rosa Parks Community Center with his wife, Jill. The painting of Parks in the background is by Carl Owens.

RIGHT Dabls with Rosa Parks on his right and Eula McClaney on his left.

Grand Detours

Every draftsman knows the difficulty of the straight line and rendering exactness. GM required that Dabls demonstrate mastery of both. But life, he says, taught him to treasure the beauty of curves.

In choosing to leave Wright's museum Dabls was no longer simply questioning his path. He had to create some answers.

He began by fashioning letters from three of his children's names into an acronym: Davida, Alake, Bakari and their shared last name of Lewis became his first muse for the bead gallery he envisioned. He slapped the letters DABLS on business cards and began circulating them. "People started calling me Dabls. It grew on me." By the time the gallery opened, he had revised the acronym to drop Lewis and include his daughter Makeda to create MBAD (Makeda, Bakari, Alake and Davida), which he continues to use interchangeably in reference to the museum and bead gallery.

He would eventually pair it with a suggestion from a frequent visitor to the early Wright Museum. A woman who changed her name to Isis after studying African culture urged him to exchange James for Olayami, a Nigerian name [pronounced O-la-yami] meaning *I am worthy of wealth*. "I knew I had to deal with this issue of being called James Lewis. It didn't mean anything. So, I went back and pulled Olayami up." Plus, he adds, jokingly, "We're in a country that insists that people have two names. I wanted mine to mean something."

53

Dabls' early gallery downtown, near the Book Cadillac building.

The changes didn't stop with his name. There was the short stint as executive director of the Rosa Parks Community Center in Detroit. Parks had made her home in Detroit since the late 1950s. Dabls met her, and they became fast friends after an early 1980s fundraiser for the museum, which featured a display of his civil rights cutout series.

Their affinity shines through in a batch of photos he's kept as proof of their friendship. She stood as the lone family member at his second wedding in 1983 when he married S. Jill Miller, a volunteer at the early Wright Museum. Parks was a star attraction during the couple's African-themed ceremony at Detroit's glitzy St. Regis Hotel. "Rosa Parks gave me away," Dabls says with a full laugh, recalling the wedding — and the marriage that ultimately ended in divorce in 2005.

The friendship continued, but the job "only lasted a couple of years because organizations with great sounding names, with no money, they're doomed to fail." However, he adds, "I wore the title well. Everyone I met, I'd say, 'Hi, I'm the executive director of the Rosa Parks Center.'"

In 1985, Dabls turned his gaze to entrepreneurship. He opened the first of two downtown Detroit galleries, essentially showrooms for his paintings, the African artifacts he started collecting, and beads. Lots of them; strands and strands. While the beauty lured him, the history moved him. "So many of the books I found talked about how beads were intertwined in the culture to communicate specific

Dabls in his gallery at the David Whitney Building in downtown Detroit. From a 1987 *Detroit Free Press* article about James Lewis and "a boutique with functional art."

information about the individual to the culture group. They began to make sense to me as a tool."

The more he read, the more he hoarded, even as traders' asking prices went skyward, up to $100 or more per strand. "I bought more than I could sell. I'd purchase beads from one trader, then he'd tell every trader on the planet, if you're in Detroit, go see Dabls."

Detroit author and storyteller Marsha Battle Philpot — also known as Marsha Music — says it was beads that also birthed a near three-decade friendship with Dabls. She met him initially as a repeat customer at his first gallery shop in the David Whitney Building. "When I found Dabls' store, I remember having this immediate sense of awe. It was obvious he was more than just a proprietor selling stuff. I wasn't an artist then, but I knew he was. Getting to know him made me want to know: How does one live an artful life?"

Dabls credits Miller-Lewis, with whom he shared three children, for launching them into business as co-owners of the Dabls Perette's Gallery. Miller-Lewis, a Howard University graduate, sold women's clothes and sponsored fashion shows. "She was the one that said, 'Let's go do our own thing.'"

For a while, the instinct paid off. "We did quite well in the business," he says. However, it didn't satisfy Dabls' cultural desires. "I still had all of this information that I spent years gathering, a working knowledge of African people, how we got

55

Creating the art on the outside of the rowhouses that make up part of the Bead Museum complex.

here, who was here before we got here and so on. I had to figure out how I could make my skill set relevant to the conditions of where we were as a culture group."

A vibrant redeveloped downtown was much talked about in the mid- to late 1980s, but in reality, it was nearly three decades away. Still there were pockets of life downtown, and each of Dabls' spaces attracted enough patrons, like Battle Philpot, to keep the doors open.

At Dabls' Bead Gallery, which would open later near the historic Book Cadillac Hotel in Detroit along Washington Boulevard, a woman named Ardie Riddick began to shop regularly and to savor listening to his stories. Over time, he told Riddick the gist of a new vision featuring his love of African material culture's purpose and his popular bead collection.

"I got it in my head to open a bead museum because I realized beads gave me a softer inroad to expose my people to African culture," he explains. "I needed to come back to the community and make whatever I was doing available to the community to emphasize things that were occurring with us prior to our enslavement."

The vision was creative but stymied by serious obstacles: the need for a space and money to acquire one. Dabls, on the other hand, was bold as ever. Riddick disclosed that she owned various properties but was struggling to keep up with the costs to maintain them. One day, he daringly asked her to agree to a land contract for the initial portion of the campus, the collection of buildings and row houses. "She freaked out. I mean, she went off on me. I'm in the store and there's people in the store. She pissed me off. So, I said, 'Just give it to me then.'"

Riddick, as Dabls recalls, walked out but not before declaring him "crazy."

THE CULTURE KEEPER

The south end of *African Scripted Language Wall*, overlooking I-96.

A week or so later, the story goes, she broke her silence with a phone call and news. "I couldn't believe it," Dabls said. She offered to donate the property to him in return for an old well-known cultural code — a handshake. "To a lot of Black people back then, a handshake had a greater value than a charge card."

Battle Philpot, the writer and friend, remembers Dabls sharing the news. "Dabls wasn't just excited to have a new place," she recalls. "He was overwhelmed that an elder would support him like that with her legacy in his hands. I mean he was *happy*."

Planetary Payback

Dabls' delight was undeniable, so was his understanding of a cautionary lesson from Aesop's fable, "The Old Man and Death." *Be careful what you wish for.*

Not long after Riddick's handshake offer, Dabls told himself a more urban version: "Man, you gotta be careful of a gift."

He adds, "I needed an attorney, a contractor, a plumber, an electrician, a whole team, and I didn't have money for any of it." Riddick died before seeing Dabls' vision start to materialize. (She is among a list of creative associates that Dabls admits losing track of due to his reclusive ways.)

The legal transfer of the deed and acquisition of the campus buildings took well over a year as his volunteer attorney, a friend, and a property company representing

Early days at the MBAD Bead Museum.

Riddick finalized the donation. "The only thing I could afford to do immediately was go board it up. I was so clueless."

Figuring out where to begin was daunting. Inevitably, Dabls circled back to art. He needed something to offset the sight of the debris and the buildings' obvious signs of deterioration. Step 1 was painting a single pattern of shapes derived from traditional mud cloth along a portion of the building that faces Grand River. He still can easily point out the exact spot he chose to paint the pattern, which is traced back to 12th century Mali, in North Africa, where it is typically dyed onto fabrics and worn by hunters as ritual protection and as a sign of status.

The more patterns he painted the more people noticed. "Once I painted the first mud cloth pattern on the first building, then other symbols, and nobody was protesting or calling the police, it dawned on me that I was using art the way my ancestors had, for a purpose, and it was communicating. People started paying more attention to what I was painting, trying to figure it out. Nobody was really noticing that the place was falling apart."

He was also energized by something he once heard Mayor Young say upon being asked about how people could help improve Detroit.

"God dammit, clean it up!"

Young's words fueled Dabls. "I didn't have a model," he says. "I had to resort back to, 'How would the Africans deal with this situation?'"

Actor Wesley Snipes visits the bead gallery's store in 2016.

He continues, "They made things happen with what was available. There wasn't any Home Depots or Lowes in the city. We had lots of material just laying around the streets of the city that I could gather and make it work."

Yet convincing friends of the future he saw was another matter. Sitting on the stoop outside the retail space with Dabls is a spring ritual for Battle Philpot. The space is one of her favorite Detroit cultural destinations partly because she witnessed its early days.

The view was pure shock. "When I finally got over to see it for the first time, and a few times after, I was like, 'What the heck? Oh no.' I felt so bad for him. What could he possibly do with this mess?"

An undeterred Dabls just kept painting, inside and outside, and straight into the city's creative landscape. "What Dabls has done isn't only about his art; it's his energy that is so welcoming," says Battle Philpot. "And he's so secure in his Blackness that he's able to attract the curiosity and support of diverse groups and bring them into the neighborhood. Dabls is a living teacher to everybody."

He concedes that his vision hasn't always been easy to share with others. Yet even that choice was an intentional one. He created a board of supporters but refused to let them get involved with the artmaking, which at the time was viewed more as graffiti-styled vandalism. "In case the city came after me, I didn't want to get anyone else involved. To me, I was using my culture, but somebody explained to me that I was really a graffiti artist. I was just bold enough to stay in one place."

Legendary Ghanaian sculptor and installation artist El Anatsui visits Dabls during a tour with a contingent of artists from the University of Michigan in Ann Arbor.

And from that one place, Dabls says he's watched many of the museum's day-to-day needs materialize into unimagined opportunities. With the $50,000 Eminent Artist prize, he can prioritize a bit of the future, starting with a roof for the vacant *Nkisi House*, which is to become a 20-room bed-and-breakfast residence space for artists. (The building is currently a gutted shell which Dabls purchased for $1,500 to save from demolition in the early 2000s.) He expects to spend at least $15,000 on the roof alone. Establishing a trust is also a priority.

Moving forward, Dabls hopes the news of the Kresge Eminent Artist Award will spur interest in his blend of African creativity and cultural resilience from a new wave of future-focused supporters.

The architectural firm LOHA's long term vision for the MBAD includes an open-air sculptured pavilion and modular gallery space within the corner building, plus walking trails. "The first phase of collaboration was very important in terms of extending Dabls' ability to engage with the community," says architect O'Her-lihy. "Still, saving the building long-intended as the actual museum is urgent."

"We need to get in there sooner rather than later to be able to stabilize it, because when you lose a roof and a floor structure, you lose the ability to stabilize those

THE CULTURE KEEPER

Dabls and director Quentin Tarantino during a 2017 visit.

walls," he says. "That's the art. We're anxious to preserve as much as we can and to help Dabls continue this wonderful story that he's spent his life telling."

O'Herlihy estimates at least $300,000 is needed to safely clear the debris inside the building, create a new foundation, stabilize the exterior walls and to design a modular gallery in its center.

The costs are big but so, too, Dabls says, is the universe's ability to surprise.

"The first people that used to come here were people touring the city waiting to see its demise," said Dabls. "But it didn't happen, and so they'd come here and see this place and say, 'Aww, this is nice. This is beautiful art.' I didn't plan that."

The compliments do bring some satisfaction, but they are secondary to his drive. "I still believe what I'm doing is having fun with history. It may look like art, but I'm not going to argue. Hell, I'm still surprised that so many people come here, and they look past all the imperfections and all the stuff that's wrong, and they still find something to connect with."

A great irony exists within the affirmation. "Been here 23 years and counting. Haven't had the money to open the actual bead museum, but no one is concerned about that but *me*."

The popularity of the museum campus — minus the actual bead museum — finally makes sense to him "because the beads I'm selling are aging in the range of two to three hundred years old, they're satisfied. I think it's clear there's things [beads] that have a history."

Ashanti beads from Ghana on display in the gallery.

Dabls still dares to believe a museum will open on his corner. His daughter Alake shares the hope. "His whole journey has been one of patience and consistency," she says. "I'm close enough to it to understand where his vision lies, why he's worked and worked at it because the beads were meant to close gaps in our history as African Americans and our culture."

Bryce Detroit holds a more spiritual wish for MBAD and Dabls. "He's been a torch showing us what it means to be rooted in your ancestry, to live connected to a legacy of millions of years of history. My hope is that this [Kresge Eminent Artists Award] will bring super resources, like over resources, to the point where we can really fortify the infrastructure so that it lasts forever, and he's here to see it happen."

These things cross his mind while he sits behind the counter inside the bead store that continues to be mistaken as the museum. He wonders about MBAD's fate but refuses to worry or push the idea that one of his children will step in to complete the museum after he's gone.

Such worries, he says, are against his culture.

"The African system says your life is your life. I can't go past my lifetime. So, I can't be sitting around with my head down, talking about, I'm not gonna have no legacy. I'm just happy that I've been able to do what I've done in my lifetime with this place and to influence some people who have crossed back into the culture with me."

Dabls in the gallery where he can be found most days.

If the MBAD African Bead Museum, or even Dabls' artwork, has any enduring meaning, he says future cultural storytellers will sift and decide. "They'll say, 'He didn't leave us any kind of narrative about what it is he was doing,'" Dabls says. "But, yes, I did leave one. It just requires a little more cultural curiosity. Nothing began with me; nothing stops with me."

NICHOLE M. CHRISTIAN is a writer and veteran journalist. She has worked as creative director, editor and lead writer for The Kresge Foundation's annual Eminent Artist monographs *A Palette for The People* (2021), honoring painter and educator Shirley Woodson; *Wonder and Flow* (2020), honoring ceramicist Marie Woo; and *A Life Speaks* (2019), honoring poet and activist Gloria House. Nichole is also coauthor of *Canvas Detroit*, and frequent essayist for M Contemporary Art, a gallery in Ferndale, Michigan.

Her writing also appears in the poetry chapbook *Cypher*, summer 2021; *Portraits 9/11/01: The Collected Portraits of Grief from The New York Times*; the online arts journal *Essay'd*; *A Detroit Anthology*; and *Dear Dad: Reflections on Fatherhood*.

"When I was called James Lewis,
I produced a lot of art. I thought
my goal was to be an artist."

Decoding the cultural and spiritual significance of Olayami Dabls' most famous installation

ANEB KGOSITSILE

Quite a few years ago, Baba[1] Dabls showed me some passages he had written about his installation, *Iron Teaching Rocks How to Rust*. Unsatisfied with his efforts to explain the work, he asked if I could do some editing for him. I did my best then to excavate his notes (their meaning was so intense), to render his vision somewhat clearer; but I hope that I have a deeper appreciation of Baba's work now, and I'm happy to offer these reflections.

Iron and iron craftsmen figure very large in African spiritual/cultural heritage. The craftsmanship of the blacksmith enables appropriation of the natural environment into patterns of spatial organization, social relationships and culture: Iron for fashioning weapons of protection, iron for tools to clear terrain, iron to harvest crops, prepare food, and create beautiful, powerful artifacts. For centuries, long before European intervention, African blacksmiths mastered a vast codification of the properties of various elements of the natural environment. This knowledge permitted them to wield both physical and metaphysical powers and secured their roles as artists and spiritual guides at the center of every village.

In Dabls' *nkisi* artwork, *Iron Teaching Rocks How to Rust*, iron symbolizes the persistence of African civilization through many centuries and numerous assaults — the Atlantic slave trade, colonialism, neocolonialism. Iron signifies the cultural traits of confidence, endurance and calm resolve through vicissitudes. Rust, iron's red residue, represents the continuity of a people's culture through generations, despite displacement. Iron teaching rocks how to rust — that is, Africans in the diaspora learning how to restore and reimagine their lives through ancestral wisdom. Such knowledge finds its way to us through deep study, as with our *griots*, and through the gift of ancestral reverence and memory. Hence Dabls' moment of inspiration:

ABOVE A view of *Protest*, part of the permanent installation on the grounds of the museum.

PREVIOUS PAGE *Detention Center*, another part of the permanent installation.

> *I saw iron lying on the ground and picked up one piece. I could feel and see why my Ancestors cultivated a physical and spiritual connection with iron and began to appreciate the beauty of this red rusted color. I noticed an iron bar protruding out from a piece of broken concrete and the rocks in the slab looked like they had rusted, but of course it was only the stain from the iron rusting. The idea was clear "iron teaching rocks how to rust."*

Dabls' entire oeuvre — the outdoor wall paintings, the central iron installation and the bead museum (for beads, as condensations of natural energy and craftsmanship, along with other material culture items, belong also to the metaphysical world) — may be experienced as one powerful architectural whole, audaciously claiming a large expanse of city land. Baba says the city has never interfered with the work. We are not surprised. Anyone would be daunted to challenge such a powerful assertion of self-determination.

---

1. *Baba* is an honorific term used in many of the cultures of southern Africa, as well as West and East Asian cultures, to demonstrate high respect for an older adult male figure.

2. In West African culture, a *griot* is a revered term for storyteller, poet or entertainer.

THE CULTURE KEEPER

Iron Teaching... is now an internationally known destination at the corner of Grand River and West Grand Boulevard! It is an *art environment* functioning as a reservoir of African spirituality, symbolism and memory. It is a prayer built of found objects, ingenuity, and African aesthetics of rich color and rhythmic design. It is an evolving collective art statement, incorporating diverse community engagements, as well as the contributions of beloved collaborators, including Detroit artists Michele Gibbs and Baba Ibn Aaron Pori Pitts. It is a repository of spiritual energies for healing and protecting a community, an extraordinary *nkisi*. African art historian Robert Farris Thompson quotes an African *griot*[2] for this definition of *nkisi*:

> *The first nkisi, called Funza, originated in God.... [It is] the thing we use to help a person when that person is sick and from which we obtain health; the name refers to leaves and medicines combined together.... An nkisi is also a chosen companion, in whom all people feel confidence. It is a hiding place for people's souls, to keep and compose in order to preserve life.* (Thompson, Flash of the Spirit. NY: Vintage Books, 1984. p. 117.)

Dabls summarizes his artistic intention, illustrating clearly the endurance of an African spiritual impulse and practice:

> *What I really hope to accomplish by creating an* nkisi *for Northwest Detroit is for our youth to have a safe passage to and from school... for our elders not to know loneliness, and for our juvenile detention centers to be so vacant that our judges and police will be bored from inactivity... that everyone takes time to listen to each other... for no home to know hunger... and for our community to once again be a family, restored and healed....*

Thank you, Baba. Asé, asé, asé ooooo!

ANEB KGOSITSILE (Gloria House, Ph.D.), Professor Emerita, University of Michigan–Dearborn and Associate Professor Emerita, Wayne State University, is a life-long freedom worker, essayist, poet, and recipient of the Lifetime Achievement Award of the Michigan Coalition for Human Rights 2017, and the Kresge Eminent Artist Award 2019.

Inside Iron

Iron Teaching Rocks How to Rust is a metaphor, the installation began in 2003. One day, I'm on the field, I was trying to figure out, "What am I going to do with all of this land out here." I picked up a rock. Really was a piece of concrete with a piece of rebar sticking out of it. But I called it a rock. I looked at it. The iron that was sticking out of this rock had stained the rock. So, I said to myself, "Oh, iron teaching rocks how to rust." I had taken an English class where the professor said, if you can think of a good title, keep it. You might be on to something.

I knew the best way to tell stories in African culture was through proverbs and metaphors. I had all this information available to me from research. What's the metaphor? Iron is teaching rocks its history.

I began to hunt for iron pieces or objects, rocks and tree branches (wood and ore are the main ingredients in making iron), iron fence posts. I saw two large 55-gallon plastic barrels lying in the field and placed them in the center of this vacant lot. We decided we would not empower others by asking for their permission or acceptance but to follow my strong desire to make this image in my mind alive. We used a tremendous amount of mirrors and mirror pieces. Consequently the visitor's image becomes part of the installation.

If by chance this project ever has to be dismantled, I wish to convey that my mission was not to create a permanent installation but to utilize the creative process and the reward was in creating this installation itself, not in the longevity.

— OLAYAMI DABLS

"I wanted to paint something that I hoped would make it to New York and I would be recognized, make a lot of money and knock Picasso off the block. But then I began to realize that that cannot be what art is about."

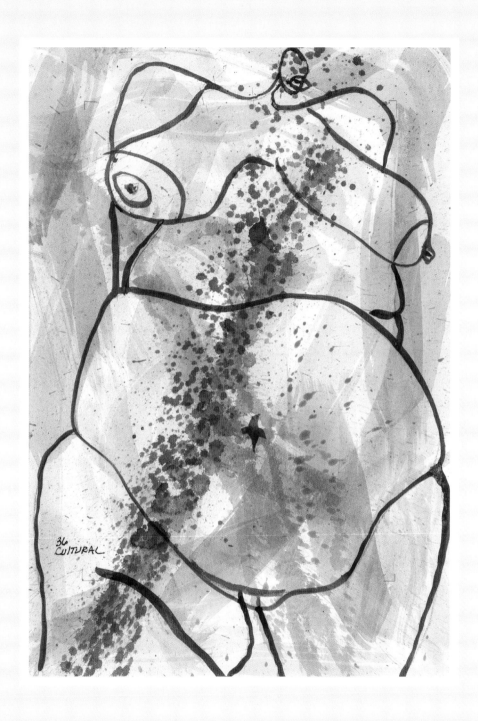

Olayami Dabls points the way to Detroit's past and its Black future

LAUREN HOOD

About a year ago, as a part of a Detroit city planning process, I facilitated a visioning session with some OGs from an east side neighborhood. To activate imagination around their Afro futures, I asked, of all the places they'd ever been to or fantasized about going to, what place topped the list and why?

Mrs. Barbara was the first to respond. "Black Bottom!" she enthusiastically declared. The Detroit Historical Society cites two identifying traits of the Black Bottom neighborhood: "predominantly Black" and "demolished for redevelopment." I asked Mrs. Barbara about her "why," even though, as a Black Detroiter and descendant of at least one grandparent and parent who resided in the neighborhood, I already knew the gist of her reasoning.

Although the physical place was long gone before my arrival in this realm, I have a relationship with it through the stories my mother tells me about the single-family dwellings turned into multiunit boarding houses where several familial generations would live and engage in a one-bedroom situation. While anxiety-inducing upon first thought, it wasn't a stretch for me to understand the benefit of cohabitating with an entire gaggle of folks who shared the same North Star: collective comeuppance. I've heard tell many times over of the communal esteem Black folks shared merely by bearing witness and being proximate to Black ownership of businesses, properties and most importantly their own outcomes.

Cultural pride is a core ingredient in the alchemy of agency. With the government sanctioned erasure of thriving Black communities like Black Bottom, gone was not only what was valuable and visible but also that which was visceral.

Dabls reflects on his work in front of *Nkisi House,* on Grand Boulevard at the Bead Museum.

FOR   US

A section of *African Scripted Language Wall.*

My first understanding of cultural pride was the experience of growing up in Coleman Young's Detroit. Being too young to witness enough of his tenure to critically question any politics, what I did know about his time at the helm was that Black folks had swagger. There was a bold Black badassness that Mayor Young embodied, and it was replicated not just by Black folks occupying the annals of power, but by 'hood folk of every distinction.

We were really feeling ourselves with that kind of representation. The audacity of showing up his whole Black self!

There are a myriad of other contributing factors to the vibration of a place, but sometime between Coleman and now, there has been a palpable shift in the energy here in Detroit. It almost feels as if there's a quieting spell cast over Black Detroiters. There will always be those who swagger on, unfazed by the cyclone of city change swirling around them, but writ large, we maintain a shadow of the Blackness that was once at the forefront of our civic identity. As Marcus Garvey states about a lack of self-knowledge, we have become like "a tree without roots" as the

THE CULTURE KEEPER

distance between us and our history, origin and culture has grown exponentially by way of survival-related distractions.

As critical to Black thriving as the universally understood "basic human needs" is Black folks' need to both know and love "thine own" culture. There are griots among us who take on the voluntary labor of cultural transmission. Dabls is one just as Coleman was. To the untuned eye, the set of buildings appears as a bead shop in its simplest form or an art installation at its best. But to the culturally curious, the Black seeker, the set of structures is something else entirely, something filled with the same spirit of Mrs. Barbara's Black Bottom.

That spirit is too complex to be reduced simply to the visibility of Black skin. It is a silent knowing born of shared hopes and slights, a passport to understandings about place(s) that *just are* (understood without explaining to other Black people). What ends up being most significant about places for people of (colored) cultural origins, can't be seen, touched or assessed for its dollar value. It's attached (hinged/ glued) to one's experience of the place and what it activates inside.

We don't inhabit places, places inhabit us.

Dabls knows this. The place that he built, the one that sits at the Grand intersection, is a place designed for the specific purpose of readying Black folks for a journey within and back to ourselves. While programming would have us believe that what we need is with(out), it's here that the African descendant storyteller turned sorcerer implores us to click our heels together three times and be "home," reminding us that the agency to get there had been within all along, having created the portal for which to be transgressed.

LAUREN HOOD is a native Detroiter. She is an occasional writer and full-time visionary. She founded and leads the Institute for AfroUrbanism which draws on Black lived experience and ancestral genius in pursuit of a thriving Black city. She's a trustee at the Charles H. Wright Museum of African American history and is the current Chairperson of the City's Planning Commission. She has been a sought-after speaker on culture, forward-thinking development and reparations.

"My first art classes, all the professors were talking about were European artists who had done great things. That stands out like a sore thumb if you've studied your own culture and have a foundation. It becomes obvious you're being indoctrinated."

THREE CUP
J. LEWIS
9-8-84

83

SYMBOL, A STORY

Culture connects beyond divides

MARION "MAME" JACKSON

Art is not simply works of art; it is the spirit that knows beauty,
that has music in its soul and the color of sunsets in its handkerchief,
that can dance on a flaming world and make the world dance too.

W.E.B. DUBOIS

Enchantment ... total enchantment!

That was my overwhelming response fifteen years ago when I first came upon an old row house on Grand River painted up in bright colors — red, black, white, yellow, green — and covered with an array of broken mirrors flashing in the mid-day sun. Traffic was light that day. I drove by slowly — and then impulsively turned at the nearest corner to return to that magical cacophony of color, which I then discovered was Olayami Dabls' MBAD African Bead Museum.

Walking into the area around the Bead Museum that day was an eye-opening experience — I had never seen anything like it before. The energy and originality of Dabls' creative environment captivated my mind and my imagination. In the grounds behind the museum, I was completely drawn in by the fascinating but puzzling sculptural installations constructed from salvaged materials — hunks of broken concrete, twisted metal, weathered slats of wood, more mirrors. My attention turned quickly to an entire house covered with patches of color, fragments of broken mirror, dozens of rusting paint can lids, and a dense web of repeated marks and forms covering what seemed to be an undulating green snake encircling the

The corner of the Bead Museum rowhouses, along Grand River Avenue.

lower level of the two-story house. I was totally absorbed by a magical, completely enveloping and transformative environment.

It was clear that Olayami Dabls was not a conventional artist. His art defies the European and Euro-American classification of artworks as unique, treasured objects to be admired for their beauty and innate value and to be viewed and protected in museums and private collections. Dabls does not aspire to have his work in a museum. Rather, he sees his role as a "storyteller" in the ancient African tradition of storytellers whose work has always been to pass forward the wisdom of earlier generations and to help center cultural values within a community. In a fantastic two-block art environment adjoining his street-front museum, Dabls has created a material realization of the stories he offers to the community. His park-like artscape is filled with sculptural installations, architectural elements and — in the spirit that stories are to be told and retold from multiple perspectives — an open-air stage for performance and public use.

The environment is engaging, lively and filled with references to ancient African spiritual traditions, as exemplified in the powerful *Nkisi House*, the old frame house covered with painted symbols and mirrors deflecting evil spirits and giving protection to African ancestors. Along the south border of Dabls' artscape is a colorful block-long wall, encrusted with fragmented mirrors and painted with archaic characters from 25 native African languages. In the largest open area, Dabls has created a group of narrative sculptural installations relating to 500 years of the African American experience.

In inventing this rich environment, Dabls is a placemaker, providing a physical environment that sparks imagination and nourishes communal experiences. His stories are not didactic and do not lead to obvious resolution. Rather they are purposely open-ended, often allegorical, and are intended to challenge viewers to come to their own conclusions about the meaning. Dabls' environment entices visitors to stop, to think, to pay attention and not be driven by habitual mental constructs supported by social norms and institutions. In short, Dabls asks visitors to be involved and, by extension, to live their own lives with energy and power.

The prevalence of fragmented mirrors and repetition of archetypal symbols of ancient Africa give a lively visual cohesiveness to Dabls' project and point to a strong spiritual center in traditional African cultures — values that Dabls feels are undervalued and lacking in today's commercialized and mechanized world. Relating ancient spiritual values of Africa and of other cultures to our present mechanized world, Dabls frequently uses the image of the snake, an animal that sheds its skin in springtime and, in African tradition, is associated with the ancestors and considered to be a symbol of rebirth, healing, and transformation.

A part of the *African Scripted Language Wall.*

The symbol of the spiral, echoing the form of a coiled snake, is often repeated in Dabls' shape-shifting environment. An archetypal symbol of continuity, the spiral supports Dabls' sense that his work draws from the primal animating spirit of the ancestors. In this sense, Dabls is a storyteller and a healer whose art sparks the imagination of visitors enabling them to see the world anew from points of view different from their own. The symbol of the spiral forms a fluid path along which individuals can find themselves moving either inward or outward from a vital source of energy. Dabls invites us to come with open minds into his mysterious art environment to experience its beauty as well as its strangeness; trusting that this unfamiliar world has something to say. The stories we hear are ultimately our own stories, hidden from us in the distant past of nations we have never known and reawakened through a sense of wonder and a new sense of possibility. Dabls' message is one for our times, at its deepest level a meditation for empowering our spirits and healing our world.

MARION "MAME" JACKSON, art historian and former chair of the Department of Art and Art History at Wayne State University, studies artistic traditions in the Americas rooted outside mainstream European traditions, particularly Inuit and Afro-Brazilian art. She is currently co-director of Con/Vida — Popular Arts of the Americas.

"I chose to figure out a way I could represent my culture with what's perceived as art. I gave up a reputation in the community because I started to realize one's name is supposed to mean more than art for art's sake."

A shared cultural love leads one artist to her voice

CHARLENE URESY

My earliest childhood memories involve drawing geometric shapes and symbols. For reasons unknown at the time, they spoke to me. Though I didn't fully understand, I stayed true to creating them even as an adult artist with African-Cuban roots.

What I didn't know about my connection to these shapes became clear to me more than 30 years ago, when I met Dabls. Through his stories and art, he helped me see the African origins at work in my work. I believe we first met at his gallery in the David Whitney Building in Detroit. From the beginning of our relationship, his purpose in life was clear to me. Dabls is here to remind African people "from which we came."

To this day, he wears this declaration proudly and surrounds himself with African material culture so that it is visible to everyone. In his own way of quiet persuasion, Dabls introduced me to the African philosophy of Ubuntu, "I am because you are."

This fundamental knowledge of connection and purposeful existence in my world has always been around, but it wasn't until a conversation with Dabls that I recognized it as an African concept. The African belief insists that everything exists by means of and in relation to all other things. I learned this from Dabls. This resolute passion in the African way and sharing it with others is what I respect most about him.

We've had so many enlightening conversations about African philosophy, religion, spirituality and music. When Dabls moved into his permanent space, he chose to paint the walls and ceiling with African symbols and cover the entire space with beads and in doing so, his purpose and his pride were amplified. Dabls designed the space for us to feel respect and wonder for African intellectual achievement.

A section of *African Scripted Language Wall* known as *Iron Sticking Out of Wood.*

HISS HANDS

A detail from the mural *Honor The African Woman Who Has Endured Colonization and Enslavement.*

The MBAD museum's aesthetic was emotionally stirring and comforting to me, taking me back to my childhood. This is where I learned the importance of my early doodling. Dabls showed me that they were African symbols like the symbols he had painted on the walls. What I was looking at was the African way of communicating through symbols, and this way is as viable as any written communication. He also convinced me that because I've been drawing these symbols since childhood this knowledge was stored deep in my DNA.

Conversations with Dabls altered the mission of my art practice. Not only would I begin to paint these symbols on repurposed furniture, but I would also do what Dabls encouraged and that is to read and research, and travel back to Cuba, something I've done for more than 20 years as part of my practice. In my research, I've learned that the symbols are called communication expressions, and the meaning of many of these symbols has been lost.

But Dabls has worked to bring back to the community what has been lost simply by sharing his knowledge, wisdom and space. Through the adornment of the facade of his building and the grounds surrounding it, you not only see Dabls as a collector but also as a storyteller, artist and muralist. *Nkisi House* and *African Scripted*

A photograph of *African Scripted Language Wall* by Charlene Uresy.

Language Wall narrate so much of what Africans contributed to the world. He is our reminder to be true to yourself and live a respectful and purposeful life. Dabls is rightly proud that he has not had any destruction on his work. The universe is looking after him.

Dabls' resolve and determination to connect us to the stories of our DNA has delivered so much to Detroit. I share Dabls' passion for making Africa's meanings real through art. As he's helped to teach me, I seek to teach others the beauty "from which we came."

CHARLENE URESY is an African-Cuban-American, self-taught artist and photographer, who was born in Chicago, Illinois, and lives in Detroit. She's been traveling to Cuba since 1999. Her mother is from Cuba and immigrated to the United States, before the Cuban Revolution. Her art of beautifully painted furniture and photography is in many private collections and her exhibition history includes North End Creators, Detroit Fine Arts Breakfast Club at Swords into Plowshares Peace Center, Souls of Black Folk and the Scarab Club. She is a board member of Mint Artist Guild, and a member of the National Conference of Artists, Detroit Fine Arts Breakfast Club and Delta Sigma Theta Sorority.

"The purpose of art is to have a
function in the culture, not what
it's become today."

A   FUTURE

Inside the renovation plans for the MBAD African Bead Museum

LORCAN O'HERLIHY

I t's always been my philosophy that architects should take on projects that are relevant to cities and contributing back. From my first meeting with Olayami Dabls it was clear to me that this is the story he's telling with his vision of a bead museum.

You can create a museum per se that's a gathering space for the community and it doesn't have to carry the weight of the old conventional white box throwing art on the walls, in a sense catering only toward the wealthy, whereas the kind of work he's doing is providing a connective tissue for the entire community.

ABOVE Axonometric view of the planned renovation.
OPPOSITE A rendering from inside the future sculpture courtyard.

ABOVE A cross-section of the museum renovation plans.

The solution we see is very much tied into Dabls' own story, his history of working with the resources that you have, and his wanting to give back in ways that connect the community through art, not very fancy materials but stuff that is enriched by art.

We have this very simple concept of inserting a prefab structure with a gallery space that would be enclosed during colder months and open air during the summer. The joy of the design is that it allows for a space that is still brought to life by murals and painting, but is responsive to all conditions, so that the bead museum becomes the true gathering space that Dabls has always envisioned.

LORCAN O'HERLIHY is founder and principal of Lorcan O'Herlihy and Associates, a Los Angeles–based architectural firm. O'Herlihy's past work includes the Louvre Extension in Paris, with I.M. Pei & Partners.

1. EXISTING CONDITIONS

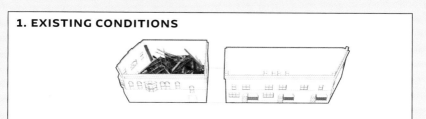

2. PREPARATION

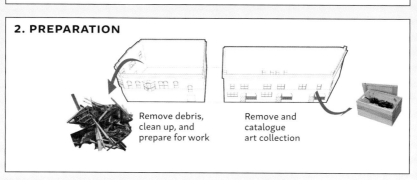

Remove debris, clean up, and prepare for work

Remove and catalogue art collection

3. REPAIR

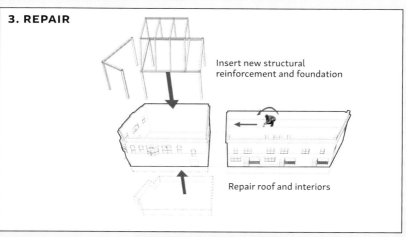

Insert new structural reinforcement and foundation

Repair roof and interiors

4. BUILD OUT

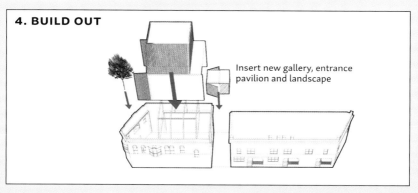

Insert new gallery, entrance pavilion and landscape

"Now, everyone wants to do art. But the rest of the planet didn't always have that word or the European model of art. The people who drew on caves 3,000 years ago weren't running around calling themselves artists. They were communicating existence, and letting the people figure out what it meant."

Select Works, Projects, and Awards

Olayami Dabls (formerly known as James Lewis)

Storyteller, Museum Curator, Art Collector, Educator, Lecturer, African Art Dealer, Founder of MBAD/ABA African Bead Museum, Co-Founder of Dabls Perrette's African Bead Gallery.

Founding member, curator and artist-in-residence of the Detroit International Afro American Sports Hall of Fame museum, Wayne County, and has created over 15,000 original art works.

Educational History

Highland Park Community College, Associate Degree, drafting technology

Chevrolet Engineering Center, drafting

Wayne State University, mechanical engineering and art

Work Experience

1998–present Founder of Dabls MBAD African Bead Museum

1996–1998 Detroit Psychiatric Institute, artist-in-residence

1993–1996 Metro Arts, artist-in-residence

1985–1990 Dabls Perrette's Gallery, part owner

1985–1988 Rosa Parks Community Center/Museum, executive director and artist-in-residence

1975–1985 Wayne County Community College District, drafting instructor

1971–1983 Charles Wright Museum of African America History, curator and artist-in-residence

Selected Awards

2016 Eco/Place By Design award, SXSW

2015 Community Art, Detroit Awesome Awards

2014 Knight Arts Challenge, Knight Foundation

2012 Kresge Artist Fellowship

Selected Exhibitions

2018 *Olayami Dabls: Absorb, Reflect, Transmit* solo installation of selected large panels made from "The Civil Rights Decade" series, Fisher Building, Detroit

2017 Saint-Etienne International Design Biennial, Saint Etienne, France

2017 ORT and the City, *Gallery of Chairs* group show, Somerset Collection, Troy, MI

2017 Art+Science Gala and Auction, MOCAD, Detroit

2017 *Detroit Grind* group show, Rush Arts Gallery, New York

2017 *Personal Space* group show, Public Pool, Hamtramck, MI

2017 *Art @ The Max* group show, Detroit Symphony Orchestra, Detroit

2016 Solo exhibition, Henry Taylor Gallery, Los Angeles

2016 *Honor of the Inaugural Beacon Project: A Photographic Salute to Makers from Detroit's Neighborhoods* group show, The Fisher Building, Detroit

2015 Solo exhibition of mirror paintings, Beaumont Health System hospital galleries, Dearborn, MI, and Taylor, MI

2015 Installation, *Nice Outfit*, part of Summer in the Park series, Paradise Valley Harmonie Park, Detroit; with Anya Sirota, U-M Architecture Faculty

2013 *Global Colors* with Jody Mitchell group show, Scarab Club, Detroit

2013 ArtX Detroit group show, MOCAD, Detroit

2013 *Vision in a Cornfield* group show, MOCAD, Detroit

2012 *Let's talk about Love, baby* group show, MOCAD, Detroit

2012 Group show, Public Pool Gallery, Hamtramck, MI

2011 Group show, INCA Gallery, Detroit

1992 Solo exhibition, First National Building Lobby, Detroit

1986 Solo exhibition, Detroit Repertory Theatre Gallery, Detroit

1985 Group show, Scarborough Gallery, Toronto, Canada

1984 *The Civil Rights Decade*, Fisher Building Lobby, Detroit

1983 Solo exhibition, Coleman A. Young Municipal Center, City/County Building, Detroit

1980 Solo exhibition, Coleman A. Young Municipal Center, City/County Building, Detroit

1979 Solo exhibition, Automobile Club of Michigan (AAA) Art Gallery, Detroit

1979 Solo exhibition, Arts Extended Gallery, Detroit

1979 Solo exhibition, Charles Wright Museum of African-American History

1978 Group show, Art Impression gallery, Detroit

1977 Solo exhibition, Plymouth Congregational Church, Detroit

Murals

2018 *Trade Beads and Snakes* mural, Grand River Avenue and Warren, City of Detroit

2017 Strategic Staffing Solutions, Penobscot Building, Detroit

2016 *Sankofa* and *Honor The African Woman Who Has Endured Colonization and Slavery*, Murals in the Market, Eastern Market, Detroit

Illustrations

1996 Sayers-Franklin, Deborah E., *Colored, Chitlins' and Coons: Dispelling the Myth of the Mammy*, Deborah E. Franklin & Assocs, Detroit

1986 Poster and set design, Dorothy Robinson Theater, Detroit

1985 Poster design and installation of sets, Dorothy Robinson Theater, Detroit

1985 Jones, Gayl, *Xarque and other poems*, Lotus Press, Detroit; cover illustrations

1984 Design and installation of theater sets, Petty Player Theater Company, Detroit

1979 Miller, S. Jill, *Dressing for Success*

Bead Museum Publications

Dabls, Olayami; Hamidi, Leila and del Sol, Corazon, eds. *The Story of Our Rights: How a Nation Moved Toward Social Justice.* MBAD African Bead Museum, Detroit, 2018

Dabls, Olayami. *African Beads: A Coloring Book.* MBAD African Bead Museum, Detroit, 1998

Unpublished Manuscripts

"Iron Teaching Rocks How to Rust," 140 pages, 100 illustrations

"Hannibal," 100 pages, 96 illustrations, oil painting

"The Civil Rights Decade," 180 pages, 165 illustrations, oil paintings

"Southern Life," 75 pages, 72 illustrations, acrylic

"Flag," 65 pages, 60 illustration, oil paintings

"African Kama Sutra," 230 pages, 225 erotic pen and ink drawings

"Catalog, MBAD/ABA Museum," 200 pages, 189 pen and ink drawings

"1967 Rebellion," 50 pages, 57 paper collages

Appearances in Periodicals

Jan. 2022 *Detroit News*, etc.
Feb. 2021 *Detroit News*
Oct. 2019 *Design Indaba*
Sep. 2018 *Detroit News*
Mar. 2018 *Vice*
Jan. 2018 *Detroit News*
May 2017 *Art21* magazine
Sep. 2016 *Art in America* magazine
Jun. 2015 *Detroit News*
Jun. 2015 *Essay'd*
Jun. 2015 *Metro Times*
Jan. 2014 *Art-magazin.de* magazine, Germany
Oct. 2014 *Elle* magazine
Feb. 2012 *Detroit News*
Jul. 2011 *B.L.A.C.* magazine
Sep. 2011 *Hour* magazine

Nov. 2011 *W* magazine
May 2009 *Detroit News*
Sep. 2009 *Washington Post*
Jul 2008 *Detroit News*
Sep. 2008 *Michigan Citizen* newspaper
Sep. 2008 *Metro Times* article
Oct. 2008 *Michigan Citizen* newspaper
Dec. 2007 *Detroit Free Press*
Jul. 2006 *Michigan Citizen* newspaper
Aug. 2006 *Michigan Citizen* newspaper
Nov 2005 *Metro Times*
Feb. 2004 *Michigan Citizen* newspaper
Oct. 2004 *African American Family*
Jun. 2003 *Michigan Citizen* newspaper
Apr. 2002 *Metro Business*
Jun. 2002 *Realtime Detroit*
Jul. 2002 *Detroit News*
Jul. 2000 *Michigan Citizen* newspaper
Jul. 1999 *Michigan Citizen* newspaper
Nov. 1999 *Metro Business*
Mar. 1998 *Metroplex* newspaper
Jul. 1997 *Detroit Free Press*
Aug. 1997 *Detroit Free Press*
Jun. 1995 *Detroit Free Press*
Feb. 1991 *Michigan Citizen* newspaper
Feb. 1988 *Detroit News*
Jul. 1988 *Art Business News*
Feb. 1987 *Caribbean Entertainment Guide*
Feb. 1987 *Michigan Chronicle*
Jun. 1987 *City Arts Quarterly*, Detroit Council of the Arts
Jul. 1987 *Summer Marygrove College Alumni Annual* magazine
Aug. 1987 *Detroit Free Press*
Nov. 1987 *Detroit Sentry* magazine
Jan. 1983 *Michigan Chronicle*
Jan. 1982 *Michigan Chronicle*
Dec. 1981 *Michigan Chronicle*
Nov. 1980 *Promenade Newscalendar*, Detroit Council of the Arts

Selected Bibliography

Sobczak, John. *A Motor City Year*, Wayne State University Press, Detroit, 2009

Hren, Stephen. *Tales from the Sustainable Underground: A Wild Journey with People*, New Society Publishers, Gabriola Island, 2011

Berardi, Francesca; Rovaldi, Antonio, illustrations. *Detour in Detroit*, Humboldt Books, Milano, 2015

Lorcan O'Herlihy Architects. *Amplified Urbanism*, Lorcan O'Herlihy Architects, Los Angeles, 2017

Video Documentaries and Appearances

2016 *How To Rust,* film by Julia Yezbick, vimeo.com/158580315#t=750s

2012 German public television

2011 *Under The Radar Michigan* program, youtu.be/KKe8SYpseqY

2011 Kresge Visual Arts Fellow documentary film, youtu.be /xYDpaD2Ny50

2011 *Unbuilding Detroit*, BBC Radio 4 program

2019 PBS NewsHour segment, https://www.pbs.org/newshour/show /this-detroit-bead-museum-honors-an -african-legacy-while-modeling -revitalization

2020 Local Axis: Dabls African Bead Museum, https://vimeo.com /444772444

Our Congratulations

Access to one's culture and history plays a significant role in personal identity and is a source of profound community connection and mutual understanding. It tethers us to the world and to each other. For hundreds of years, African Americans had no direct access to the cultures and histories from which they came, particularly traditional material culture. This absence was felt deeply by 2022 Kresge Eminent Artist Olayami Dabls, whose work as a visual storyteller, placemaker, muralist, and educator has altered the physical and psychological landscape of Detroit to the benefit of all.

"If you mimic or assimilate to someone else's culture, then your own culture deteriorates," says Dabls who, for more than 45 years, has dedicated himself to uplifting and celebrating African material culture as a way of connecting to, and communicating with, ancestral lives, traditions, and stories. As founder and curator of the MBAD African Bead Museum — a massive campus housing a sculpture garden with 18 outdoor installations, the African Bead Gallery, *Nkisi House* and the 150-foot *African Scripted Language Wall* — Dabls created a vibrant and powerful symbol of Detroit, a creative community, and a beacon for thousands of visitors from around the world.

Founded in 1998, the MBAD African Bead Museum radically departed from typical museum practice. By inviting visitors to physically engage with its abundant examples of African cultural production — to touch and to hold history spanning hundreds of years — Dabls presented a model of community access and culture-sharing that to this day remains both rare and at the leading edge of what museums can and should be.

The MBAD African Bead Museum offers all who enter an undistorted African lens through which to understand African American art and experience. It also serves as a gateway to Dabls' vision as artist and creator of thousands of original works of art, including paintings, installations, jewelry, sculptures, and murals at Eastern Market and across the city. Among the well-deserved accolades for his extensive body of work is a 2011 Kresge Artist Fellowship, the $25,000 application-based award given annually to metro Detroit artists across disciplines.

Dabls' aesthetic exists along a continuum between the past and present that includes self-creation and self-definition, as well as honoring and building upon the work of the ancestors. It is also a path toward healing oneself and one's community.

We are pleased to spotlight and celebrate the vision, dedication, and impact of Olayami Dabls with the 2022 Kresge Eminent Artist Award.

CHRISTINA DeROOS
DIRECTOR, KRESGE ARTS IN DETROIT

The Kresge Eminent Artist Award, a $50,000 no-strings-attached prize, is administered for The Kresge Foundation by the Kresge Arts in Detroit office of the College for Creative Studies. We extend our sincere appreciation to this year's panelists for their work in selecting the 2022 Kresge Eminent Artist.

Our Congratulations

Recognizing Olayami Dabls' enduring career as a visual storyteller, muralist and creative placemaker, makes his selection to receive the 2022 Kresge Eminent Artist Award irrefutable.

Detroit has an extremely rich heritage of public art, which adds an enormous value to our cultural, aesthetic and economic vitality as a city. It's accessible to all, engages social interaction and tells a story — it's a direct reflection of its time and place and inspires people to observe on a deeper level and think more about the environments that we occupy.

For decades, Dabls has been transforming two city blocks into a communal space for understanding through his own sculptural work and his collection of African material culture. The MBAD African Bead Museum is not only a vibrant destination for visitors from all around the world, but also a place of education — helping the community understand the immense power of their African heritage.

Every inch of MBAD is rich with story and connects our community and its visitors to a time and place. It is part of the imperative public arts infrastructure in Detroit and Dabls' commitment to providing the community an immersive, connected space and experience. It is an honor to administer Kresge Arts in Detroit on behalf of The Kresge Foundation, and to celebrate Olayami Dabls as the 2022 Kresge Eminent Artist.

DON TUSKI
PRESIDENT, COLLEGE FOR CREATIVE STUDIES

The Kresge Eminent Artist Award

The 2022 Kresge Eminent Artist Selection Committee

Olayami Dabls was chosen as the 2022 recipient of the Kresge Eminent Artist Award by a distinguished group of artists and arts professionals.

MICHAEL HODGES Fine arts writer and author of *Building the Modern World, Albert Kahn in Detroit*

DEBRA WHITE-HUNT Dancer and co-founder and artistic director of Detroit-Windsor Dance Academy and 2020 Kresge Artist Fellow

KEITH OWENS Journalist, cultural critic and independent publisher

SATORI SHAKOOR Actress, founder of *The Secret Society of Twisted Storytellers*, host of *Detroit Performs: Live from Marygrove* and 2017 Kresge Artist Fellow

S. KAY YOUNG Artist, activist and photographer

The Kresge Eminent Artist Award

Established in 2008, the Kresge Eminent Artist Award honors an exceptional literary, fine, film or performing artist whose influential body of work, lifelong professional achievements and proven, continued commitment to the Detroit cultural community are evident.

The Kresge Eminent Artist Award celebrates artistic innovation and rewards integrity and depth of vision with the financial support of $50,000. The Kresge Eminent Artist Award is unrestricted and is given annually to an artist who has lived and worked in Wayne, Oakland or Macomb counties for a significant number of years. The Kresge Eminent Artist Award, annual Kresge Artist Fellowships, Gilda Awards, and multiyear grants to arts and cultural organizations in metropolitan Detroit constitute Kresge Arts in Detroit, the foundation's core effort to provide broad support to the regional arts community. The College for Creative Studies administers the Kresge Eminent Artist Award on behalf of The Kresge Foundation.

About The Kresge Foundation

The Kresge Foundation was founded in 1924 to promote human progress. Today, Kresge fulfills that mission by building and strengthening pathways to opportunity for low-income people in America's cities, seeking to dismantle structural and systemic barriers to equality and justice. Using a full array of grant, loan and other investment tools, Kresge invests more than $160 million annually to foster economic and social change.

Publication Team

JENNIFER KULCZYCKI Director, External Affairs & Communications

JULIE A. BAGLEY Communications Assistant, External Affairs & Communications

W. KIM HERON Senior Communications Officer, External Affairs & Communications

ALEJANDRO HERRERA Senior Graphic Designer, External Affairs & Communications

Creative Team

NICHOLE CHRISTIAN Creative Director, Editor & Lead Writer

PATRICK BARBER Art Director & Photographer

Previous Kresge Eminent Artist Award Recipients

Shirley Woodson, 2021

Marie Woo, 2020

Patricia Terry-Ross, 2017

Leni Sinclair, 2016

David DiChiera, 2013

Naomi Long Madgett, 2012

PATRICK BARBER

NOAH ELLIOTT MORRISON

Gloria House, 2019

Wendell Harrison, 2018

ELLY STEWART

MICHELLE ANDONIAN

Ruth Adler Schnee, 2015

Bill Rauhauser, 2014

PAUL DAVIS

JUSTIN MACONOCHIE

NICK SOUSANIS

Bill Harris, 2011

Marcus Belgrave, 2009

Charles McGee, 2008

Index

This index is sorted letter-by-letter. Italic page locators indicate photographs on the page.

List of works

Photo and Image Credits

Unless otherwise noted, photos used throughout this monograph are from the personal collection of Olayami Dabls. Every effort has been made to locate and credit the holders of copyrighted materials.

Archie, William, for the Detroit Free Press. 55

Barber, Patrick. Cover and spine. 2–3, 4–5, 8–9, 10–11, 12, 14–15, 17, 19, 20, 23, 24–25, 26–27, 34–35, 57, 58–59, 64, 65, 66–67, 70, 72, 74–75, 79, 80, 84, 91, 92, 102–103, 107, 108–109, 110–111, 112, 118–119, 124–125

Courtesy of LOHA. 21, 96, 97, 98, 99

Uresy, Charlene. 93

THE CULTURE KEEPER

Requests to reproduce material from this work
should be sent to:

THE KRESGE FOUNDATION
3215 W. Big Beaver Rd.
Troy, Michigan 48084
media@kresge.org

TYPE
Fern Text Variable body text
Skolar Sans Latin Extended small text & sidebars
ALFARN and **Alfarn 2** titles
New Spirit large text & decks
Ohno Fatface punctuational **"assistance"**

Printed and bound by KTD Print

THE CREATIVE TEAM offers our utmost thanks to
Olayami Dabls for his generosity of time and a mesmerizing
series of guided outdoor tours despite far too many bitterly
cold and snowy Saturday mornings. Your good humor
enlivened each experience and the creation of this work.

We extend sincere thanks as well to Lauren Hood, Aneb
Kgositsile (Gloria House, Ph.D.), Marion "Mame" Jackson,
Lorcan O'Herlihy and Charlene Uresy for their creative
spirit and contributions.

Complimentary copies of this monograph and others in the
Kresge Eminent Artist series are available while supplies
last. All monographs are also available for download.

Visit **kresge.org/news-views/kresge-eminent-artists/**
or scan the QR code at right for more information.